Digesting
Food

Richard Walker

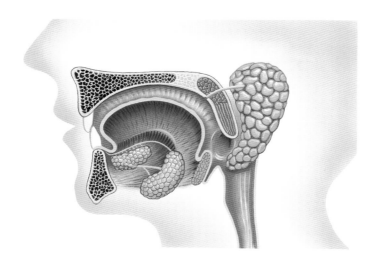

W

FRANKLIN WATTS
LONDON·SYDNEY

First published in 2004 by Franklin Watts
96 Leonard Street, London EC2A 4XD

Franklin Watts Australia
45–51 Huntley Street
Alexandria, NSW 2015

Series editor: Adrian Cole
Series design: White Design
Art director: Jonathan Hair
Picture research: Diana Morris
Educational consultant: Peter Riley
Medical consultant: Dr Gabrielle Murphy

A CIP catalogue record for this book is available from the British Library.

ISBN: 0 7496 5136 9

Printed in Malaysia

Acknowledgements:

BSIP Laurent/H. Americain/SPL: 25b. Ian Boddy/SPL: 27c. Mike
Chew/Corbis: 21b. A.B. Dowsett/SPL: 22tr. Chris Fairclough: 11c&b.
Owen Franken/Corbis: 22bl. Dr Gary Gaugler/SPL: 19c. Gusto/SPL: 21t.
Wolfgang Kaehler/Corbis: 23t. Jutta Klee/Corbis: front cover, 4t.
Professors P. Motta & F. Magliocca / University "La Sapienza",
Rome/SPL: 19t. Professors P.M. Motta, K.R. Porter, & P.M.
Andrews/SPL: 14b. Susumu Nishinaga/SPL: 12b, 17c. Dr K.F.R.
Schiller/SPL: 15c. J.W. Shuler/SPL: 4b. SPL: 11t, 15b, 26bl, 26bc.
Sinclair Stammers/SPL: 9b. Hattie Young/SPL: 27t.

Every attempt has been made to clear copyright.
Should there be any inadvertent omission, please
apply to the publisher for rectification.

Contents

The body processes the
food we eat

Two, three or more times each day, we stop what we are doing and eat food. We do not just do this because we are hungry, or because the food looks or smells so good. The real reason is that we need food to stay alive. And the body processes food to make sure we can use it to best effect.

Eating to live

Eating food is both enjoyable and essential to keep us alive and healthy.

Why eat?

The average person eats about 20 tonnes of food in a lifetime. Food provides the energy needed to keep the trillions of tiny living cells that make up the body alive and active. Food also provides us with all the raw materials necessary for the body to grow and repair itself.

What is digestion?

We would not be able to make any use of food without the process of digestion. The nutrients (see pages 6–7) in food are essential for life. But they are trapped inside food so the body cannot use them. Digestion breaks down food and releases the nutrients. These are absorbed (taken up) into the bloodstream and taken to the cells. Any waste left behind passes through and out of the body. Eating, digestion, absorbing and getting rid of waste is the job of the digestive system.

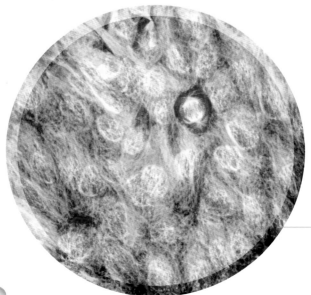

Hungry cells

Digestion makes nutrients available to the body cells, like the ones shown here, so they can stay alive.

Food processor

At the centre of the digestive system is a long tube – about 9 metres long – called the alimentary canal. It is divided up into different parts – the mouth, pharynx, oesophagus, stomach, small intestine, large intestine – each with its own digesting job. To help the process of digestion the teeth, tongue, salivary glands, liver, gall bladder and pancreas work with the alimentary canal.

FEELING HUNGRY

You do not have to remind yourself about eating food. Your brain does it for you automatically. It keeps track of how much food is being carried by the blood to your cells. If the level drops, it makes you feel hungry. Keep a diary over two or three days and record each time you feel hungry. Compare your results with those of your friends.

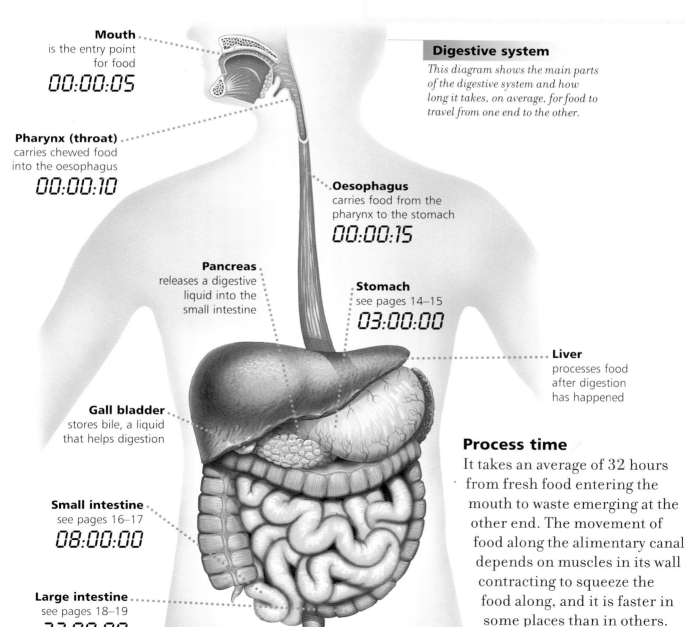

Mouth
is the entry point
for food
00:00:05

Pharynx (throat)
carries chewed food
into the oesophagus
00:00:10

Oesophagus
carries food from the
pharynx to the stomach
00:00:15

Pancreas
releases a digestive
liquid into the
small intestine

Stomach
see pages 14–15
03:00:00

Digestive system

This diagram shows the main parts of the digestive system and how long it takes, on average, for food to travel from one end to the other.

Liver
processes food
after digestion
has happened

Gall bladder
stores bile, a liquid
that helps digestion

Small intestine
see pages 16–17
08:00:00

Large intestine
see pages 18–19
32:00:00

Process time

It takes an average of 32 hours from fresh food entering the mouth to waste emerging at the other end. The movement of food along the alimentary canal depends on muscles in its wall contracting to squeeze the food along, and it is faster in some places than in others.

Food is made up of **different nutrients**

Food provides the body with nutrients, the substances it needs to work normally. There are seven different types of nutrient: carbohydrates, proteins and fats make up most of what we eat; vitamins and minerals are only needed in tiny amounts but are still essential; water makes up over half of the body; and fibre keeps the digestive system working properly.

Carbohydrates

These provide the main energy supply for the body. They occur in two main forms – starch and sugars. Starch is made up of large molecules and needs to be digested before the body can use it. Starch is found in foods such as potatoes, bread and pasta. Sugars, such as glucose, taste sweet and occur naturally in fruits. Body cells use glucose as their main source of energy (see page 20).

(see page 20)

Starch

These foods are rich in a carbohydrate called starch. Other foods, such as apples, are rich in another form of carbohydrate called sugars.

Fats

Fats are very rich in energy and they give us a long-term energy reserve of body fat, which is stored under the skin. This also helps to insulate the body and stop it from losing heat. Foods that are rich in fats include dairy products, meat, eggs and oily fish (such as mackerel).

Very rich in energy

Fats come in a variety of forms, and in small amounts are essential for a healthy body.

READING THE PACKET

In many countries, food companies print information on the packet or tin about the exact nutrient content of the food – as well as how much energy it contains (see pages 20–21). Some companies also include information about the vitamins and minerals. To find out more about the nutrient content of food, have a look at the information panel on some food packaging, like the one on the right from a cereal packet.

	per 100g	Serving of 30g*
Energy	1551kJ	719kJ
	366 kcal	170 kcal
Protein	8.1g	6.7g
Carbohydrate	74.6g	28.5g
of which: sugars	21.2g	12.2g
Fat	3.9g	3.2g
of which: saturates	1.2g	1.5g
Fibre	6.5g	2g
Sodium (salt)	0.8g	0.3g

*with 125ml semi-skimmed milk

Vitamins and minerals

Vitamins include vitamins A, C, D and E, and the B group of vitamins. Vitamin A, for example, is needed for normal vision. It is found mainly in carrots and dark green vegetables, peaches and oily fish. Minerals include calcium, which is needed for healthy bones and teeth. Calcium is found mainly in milk and dairy products.

Rich in fibre

Fruit and vegetables are rich in fibre. Many also contain essential vitamins and minerals.

Proteins

Proteins are used by the body for many different purposes including building skin and hair, and for growth and repair. Foods that are rich in proteins include fish, meat, beans, nuts and eggs.

Body builders

These foods are all good sources of protein. Many also contain fats and oils.

Water and fibre

Apart from the water we drink, most food also contains water. Water makes up over half the human body, and is essential for cells to work properly. Fibre consists of the parts of plant foods that cannot be digested. It makes the muscles of the intestines work harder at pushing the food along so they become more efficient.

Food is digested so it can be
used by the body

The digestive system works like a production line in reverse. Instead of building parts up to make a finished product, it breaks a product down into its smaller parts. It does this in two ways. First the digestive system grinds and crushes food into small pieces. Then it breaks down the pieces into simple nutrients using special chemicals called enzymes.

Crush and grind

From something that looks attractive, food is cut, sliced, ground, churned and squashed into a creamy, mushy paste of tiny particles. This is achieved by the action of the teeth and the muscular walls of the stomach. This action allows enzymes to work efficiently and to break food down completely.

From solid to liquid

This blender reduces food to smaller particles just like the action of the upper digestive system.

1. Large food molecule
meets up with an enzyme

Enzyme
speeds up the breakdown of the large food molecule

2. Food molecule
slots into the enzyme and begins to break down

3. Smaller food molecules
move away from the unchanged enzyme

Enzymes at work

This sequence of pictures shows how an enzyme works.

Chemical digesters

Enzymes play a vital role in digestion. They are chemicals that are released in fluid into the mouth, stomach and small intestine, which speed up the breakdown of foods into simple nutrients. The individual food molecule fits into the enzyme like a key in a lock. The food molecule splits into smaller molecules, leaving the enzymes unchanged and ready to work again.

After the breakdown

Complex carbohydrate molecules, such as starch, are broken down into simpler sugars, such as glucose. Proteins are broken down into their building blocks called amino acids, which the body uses to build new proteins. Fats are broken down into fatty acids. These simple nutrients can be absorbed into the body through the small intestine.

Outside digestion

Not all animals digest their food inside their bodies. When flies land on their food, for example, they squirt saliva onto it. This contains enzymes that break down the food and turn it into a mush, which the fly then sucks in through its mouthparts. While doing so, it leaves behind germs, which is why food should be covered until it is ready to be eaten.

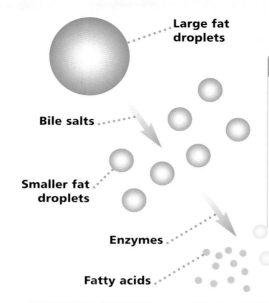

Large fat droplets

Bile salts

Smaller fat droplets

Enzymes

Fatty acids

Monoglycerides

Simple nutrients

This illustration shows how fat is broken down into simple nutrients (fatty acids and monoglycerides) by bile salts from the liver and enzymes produced by the stomach, liver and pancreas.

ENZYMES AT WORK

Find out for yourself the effects of enzymes at work. Take a piece of white bread, bite off a piece and start chewing it. At first it does not taste of very much because it is mostly made up of starch. But the saliva (spit in your mouth) contains an enzyme that breaks down starch into sugars. Chew for a few minutes and you will start to detect a sweet taste as the sugars build up.

Fly feeding
Flies, like this one, digest their food by throwing up enzyme-rich saliva onto it.

Teeth start off the
process of digestion

Teeth are hard and strong, and are found in curved rows in the top and bottom of the mouth. Teeth just behind the lips grab food and bite off pieces that will fit in the mouth. The ones further back crush and chew food into pieces that are small enough to be swallowed.

Slicers and crushers

There are four different types of teeth, each with its own job. At the front of the mouth, sharp-edged incisors slice food into chewable chunks. Pointed canine teeth grip food and pierce it. Broad, flat premolars and molars grind and crush food into a paste.

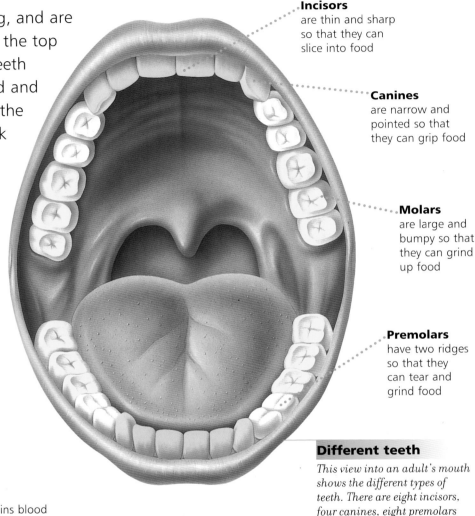

Incisors
are thin and sharp so that they can slice into food

Canines
are narrow and pointed so that they can grip food

Molars
are large and bumpy so that they can grind up food

Premolars
have two ridges so that they can tear and grind food

Different teeth
This view into an adult's mouth shows the different types of teeth. There are eight incisors, four canines, eight premolars and twelve molars.

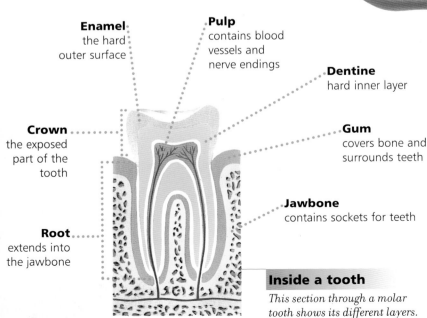

Enamel
the hard outer surface

Pulp
contains blood vessels and nerve endings

Dentine
hard inner layer

Crown
the exposed part of the tooth

Gum
covers bone and surrounds teeth

Jawbone
contains sockets for teeth

Root
extends into the jawbone

Inside a tooth
This section through a molar tooth shows its different layers.

Tooth structure

The part of a tooth above the gum is called the crown, while the part fixed into a socket in the jawbone is called the root. The crown is covered by enamel, the hardest substance in the body. Bone-like dentine forms the tooth's framework. The inner soft pulp cavity contains blood vessels and nerve endings that allow us to detect pressure when chewing, as well as heat, cold and pain.

REVEALING PLAQUE

Ask an adult to get some plaque disclosing tablets from a pharmacy. Under adult supervision, chew one of the tablets. It will stain your teeth where they are coated with plaque. Now carefully brush your teeth. How much of the plaque still remains? How good is your tooth brushing?

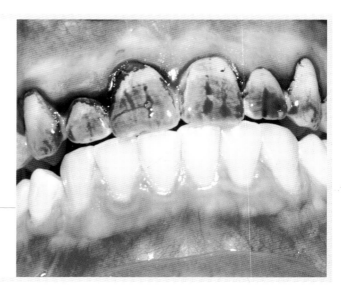

Clean teeth?

Stained areas show where teeth are coated with bacteria-packed plaque.

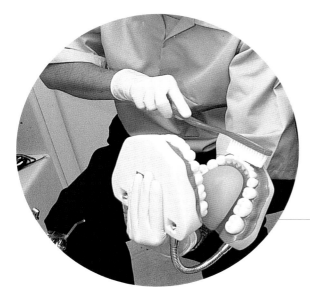

Tooth decay

If teeth are not brushed properly they become covered with a sticky layer of bacteria and food, called plaque. As bacteria feed on the food (especially sugary sweets and soft drinks), they release acids that dissolve away, or decay, tooth enamel. If tooth decay is not treated, the acids can tunnel away into the dentine or even the pulp. This causes a lot of pain, and can make teeth rot and fall out.

Careful brushing

If we look after our teeth by following dentists' advice our adult teeth should last a lifetime.

Under attack

The x-ray photograph on the computer screen helps the dentist to identify potential problems inside the teeth.

Two sets of teeth

We have two sets of teeth during our lifetime. The first set of 20 teeth, called milk teeth, starts to push through the gums when a child is about six months old. The second set of 32 teeth, called adult teeth, develops below the milk teeth. Between the ages of six and 14 the adult teeth gradually appear and push the milk teeth out.

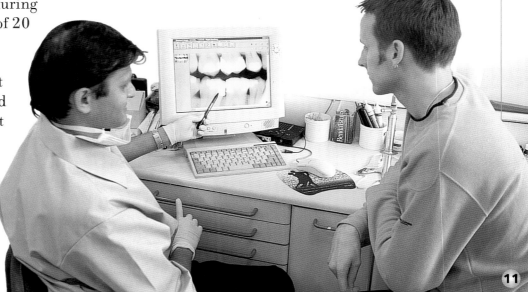

Food is chewed in the mouth and
then swallowed

Once food gets inside the mouth it is sprayed with slimy saliva, tasted by the tongue and crushed by the teeth. The tongue mixes up the ground-up food and pushes a lump of it into the throat. This is automatically squeezed down a tube that leads to the stomach.

Salivary glands

About 1.2 litres of saliva is released daily from three pairs of glands in the bottom of the mouth and in front of the ear.

Squirting saliva

The sight, smell, or even the thought of food causes lots of saliva to be squirted into the mouth. Saliva helps to moisten food and contains slimy mucus. This makes food easier to swallow. Saliva also contains an enzyme that helps break down starch.

Food grippers

These spiky projections, called papillae, allow the tongue to grip food during chewing. Other papillae house taste sensors.

Teeth
cut and crush food into small pieces

Hard palate
forms the roof of the mouth

Tongue
moves food around during chewing

Soft palate
stops food going up the nose during chewing

Pharynx (throat)
the tube that carries food from the mouth to the oesophagus

Salivary glands
release saliva into the mouth

Oesophagus
the tube that carries chewed food to the stomach

Tongue at work

The muscular tongue moves food between the teeth during chewing, making sure that each bit is crushed. It also mixes chewed food with saliva, forming a squashy, slimy ball. Taste sensors on the tongue tell us whether food is salty, sweet, sour or bitter.

Chewing muscles

Two powerful muscles – called the masseter and temporalis – pull the movable bone of the jaw (the lower jaw) upwards towards the immovable part (the upper jaw). These powerful muscles create an incredible biting force so that the teeth can grind up food.

Swallowing

Once food has been reduced to a mush, it is ready to swallow. This moves food from the mouth to the stomach and takes only a few seconds. It is usually divided into three stages. The first stage is under our control, but the other two are automatic.

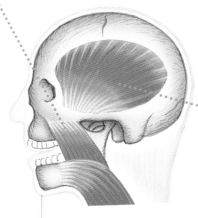

Masseter
pulls the lower mandible (jaw) upwards with great force

Temporalis
helps the masseter to close the mouth

Jaw pullers
This shows the positions of the masseter and the temporalis muscles.

Stage 1
The tongue pushes food backwards into the pharynx (throat). The soft palate rises to stop food going up the nose.

Stage 2
Food is pushed down the throat, while a 'trapdoor' called the epiglottis closes the entrance to the windpipe to stop food entering the lungs.

Stage 3
Waves of muscle contraction, called peristalsis, push the food ball down the oesophagus, the tube that links the pharynx (throat) to the stomach.

PERISTALSIS

To see how peristalsis works, take a long sock and a tennis ball. Put the tennis ball inside one end of the sock. Hold the end of the sock with one hand, while making a ring just behind the ball with the fingers of the other hand. Now squeeze with the finger ring to push the ball along the sock. This squeezing represents a wave of contraction of the smooth muscles in the wall of the oesophagus.

Peristalsis
Muscles relax (2) and contract (1) forming a wave-like action called peristalsis. The food ball is gradually squeezed into the stomach.

The stomach turns chewed food into
a creamy liquid

A few seconds after it is swallowed, food arrives in a stretchy, muscular bag called the stomach. Here food is churned up into a creamy liquid called chyme. The stomach also stores food for three or more hours, then releases it slowly and steadily into the next part of the digestive system.

Muscular bag

When empty, the stomach is no bigger than a fist, but when full it can increase in size by up to 20 times. Its stretchy wall contains three layers of muscles that contract (pull) powerfully in different directions to churn and mix up the food thoroughly. The stomach's lining is folded when empty. These folds disappear as the stomach fills with food. A ring of muscle, called the pyloric sphincter, closes off the exit from the stomach into the small intestine.

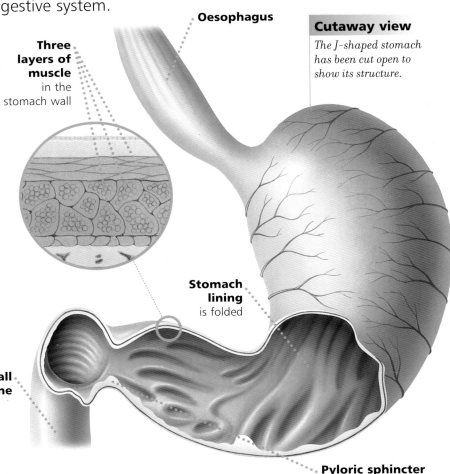

Oesophagus

Three layers of muscle in the stomach wall

Cutaway view
The J-shaped stomach has been cut open to show its structure.

Stomach lining is folded

Small intestine

Pyloric sphincter opens and closes the exit from the stomach

Gastric gland
This micrograph shows the opening of a gastric gland in the stomach lining.

Stomach juice

When food arrives in the stomach, millions of tiny glands in the stomach's wall produce a liquid called gastric (stomach) juice. Gastric juice contains powerful hydrochloric acid, which kills most harmful bacteria in food (see page 23), and the enzyme pepsin, which digests proteins. Gastric juice also contains mucus that covers the stomach's lining and stops it from being digested by its own pepsin.

Filling and emptying

When food arrives in the stomach it is processed in three stages that together can last between three and six hours. This depends on how fatty the food is and the size of the meal.

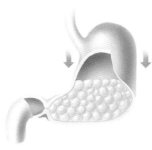 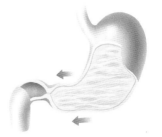 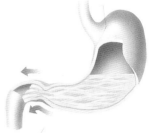

Filling
Waves of muscle contractions mix gastric juice with mushy balls of soft food arriving from the mouth.

Digesting
Strong contractions churn the mixture of gastric juice and food into a creamy liquid called chyme.

Emptying
When the chyme has been liquified completely, the pyloric sphincter relaxes slightly to allow squirts of food to pass into the small intestine.

Slimy lining
Taken using an endoscope, this image shows the pyloric sphincter of a living person. Like other parts of the digestive system, it is covered with slimy mucus.

Burping and vomiting

If too much air is swallowed during eating or drinking, the stomach walls contract to push the air upwards and out of the mouth. The noise the air makes as it leaves the mouth is called burping. When someone vomits it is often the result of overeating, bad food or various other causes. During vomiting, muscles push food in the reverse direction up the oesophagus and out of the mouth and nose.

HUMAN EXPERIMENT

In 1822 an American fur trapper called Alexis St Martin accidentally shot himself in the side. His life was saved by army surgeon William Beaumont, but the injury left a permanent opening to Alexis' stomach. Dr Beaumont used this to conduct experiments about digestion in the stomach, and made many discoveries.

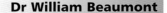

Dr William Beaumont
This American doctor carried out experiments to discover how digestion in the stomach happens.

Digestion is completed in the
small intestine

The small intestine is the long tube that runs from the stomach to the large intestine. As food passes along the small intestine, it is broken down into very simple nutrients. These nutrients then pass into the bloodstream and are carried to all the body's cells.

Small intestine

The small intestine is the longest part of the digestive system – as long as two cars placed end to end. It has three sections: the duodenum, jejunum and ileum. The first section, the short duodenum, receives chyme from the stomach and starts to digest it. The jejunum releases lots of enzymes that complete the digestion process. The ileum, the third and longest part, absorbs nutrients into the bloodstream, leaving just the waste that goes on to the large intestine.

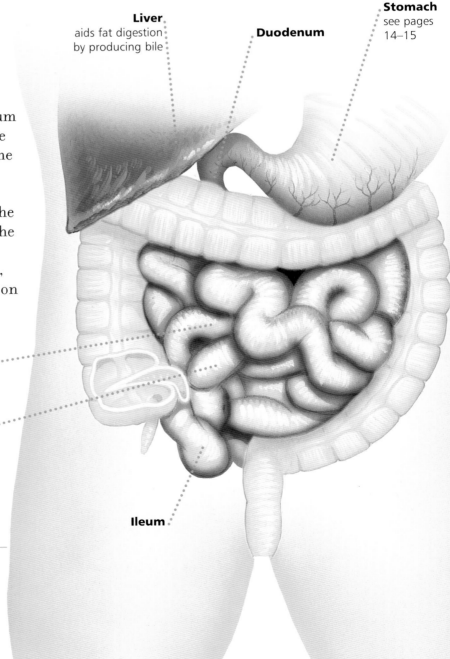

Liver
aids fat digestion
by producing bile

Duodenum

Stomach
see pages
14–15

Jejunum

Small intestine
is divided into
the duodenum,
jejunum
and ileum

Ileum

Packed in

The 6.5 metre-long small intestine is folded and coiled to fit inside the abdomen.

Pancreas and liver

These two organs greatly help digestion in the small intestine. The pancreas makes enzymes that digest starch, proteins and fats, and releases them to do their work in the duodenum. The liver – the largest internal organ in the body – produces a green liquid called bile, which is stored in a bag called the gall bladder and then squirted into the duodenum. Bile breaks fats into tiny droplets that are easier to digest.

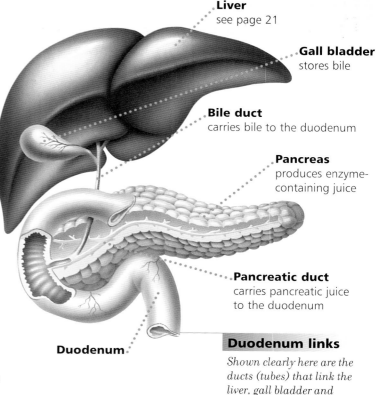

Liver
see page 21

Gall bladder
stores bile

Bile duct
carries bile to the duodenum

Pancreas
produces enzyme-containing juice

Pancreatic duct
carries pancreatic juice to the duodenum

Duodenum

Duodenum links
Shown clearly here are the ducts (tubes) that link the liver, gall bladder and pancreas to the duodenum.

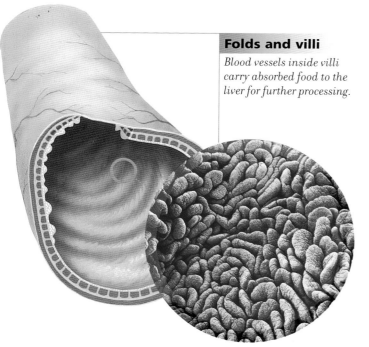

Folds and villi
Blood vessels inside villi carry absorbed food to the liver for further processing.

Inside the small intestine

The folded inner lining of the small intestine is covered with millions of tiny finger-like projections called villi. These villi, no more than 1 millimetre long, provide a massive surface for taking in (absorbing) the nutrients – such as glucose, amino acids and fatty acids – produced by digestion in the small intestine.

DIGESTING PROTEINS

This activity investigates how proteins are digested, in a similar way to the process that occurs in the small intestine. Take two pieces of the same material, stain them with tomato ketchup and allow them to dry. Take two glasses of warm water. Ask an adult to add biological (enzyme-containing) washing powder to one, and nonbiological powder to the other. Now, ask them to put one piece of material in each glass. The stain in the biological powder fades first because the enzymes in the powder break down the proteins that produce the stain's colour.

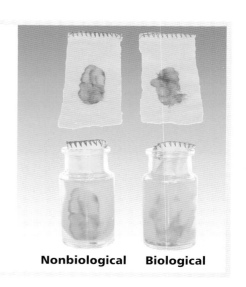

Nonbiological   **Biological**

The large intestine gets rid of waste and
saves water

The large intestine receives watery waste from the small intestine. This waste contains food, such as fibre, that could not be digested. As waste passes along the large intestine, water is absorbed back into the blood. This process turns the liquid waste into more solid faeces. Faeces are pushed out through the anus when we go to the toilet.

Large and small

The large intestine (above, bottom: 1.5 metres long) is much shorter than the small intestine (above, top: 6.5 metres long), but it is much wider, giving it the name 'large'.

Large intestine

The large intestine has three parts: the short caecum, the colon and the rectum. As waste makes its 12- to 32-hour journey along the colon, the main part of the large intestine, it is turned into faeces. These contain undigested food — especially fibre from plant foods — as well as bacteria and dead cells. When faeces reach the rectum, a person feels the urge to go to the toilet. The two sphincters (rings of muscle) around the anus — the opening to the outside — are relaxed and the faeces pushed out.

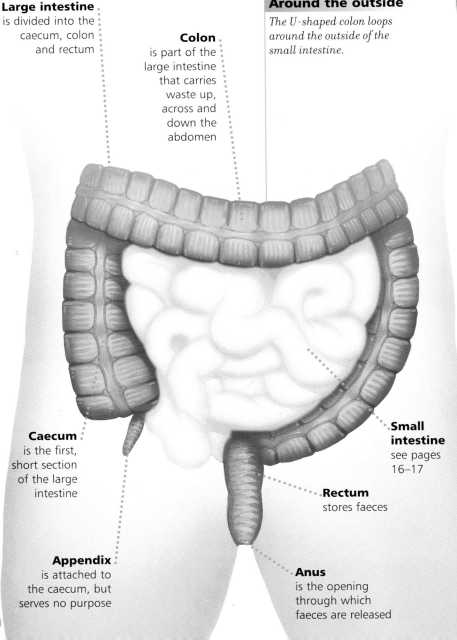

Large intestine
is divided into the caecum, colon and rectum

Colon
is part of the large intestine that carries waste up, across and down the abdomen

Around the outside
The U-shaped colon loops around the outside of the small intestine.

Caecum
is the first, short section of the large intestine

Small intestine
see pages 16–17

Rectum
stores faeces

Appendix
is attached to the caecum, but serves no purpose

Anus
is the opening through which faeces are released

Saving water

Cells lining the colon perform a vital job. They take in water from waste and recycle it back into the bloodstream. This makes sure the body does not lose water too quickly and become dehydrated. If the colon cannot absorb water properly, perhaps because it is infected or inflamed, faeces become very watery. This is called diarrhoea.

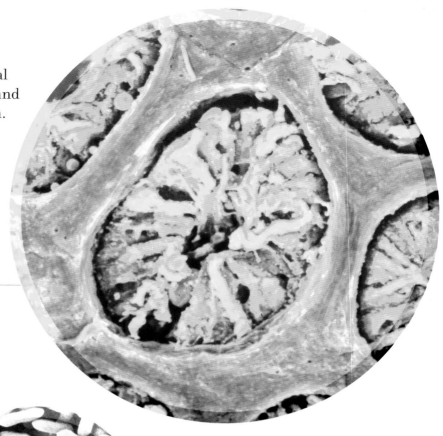

Water absorbers

This micrograph of the colon lining shows the cells that absorb water as well as glands that release slimy mucus, which smoothes the passage of the faeces.

Colon bacteria

This micrograph shows some of the bacteria that live inside the large intestine.

Friendly bacteria

The colon contains many more bacteria than there are cells in the body. They digest undigested food, at the same time releasing the smelly gases found in farts. They also release useful nutrients, such as vitamin K, that are used by the body.

LISTENING TO DIGESTION

Use a tape recorder and microphone to record the sounds made by your and your friends' intestines. Doctors call these sounds 'borborygmi', a word that sounds like the digestive noises themselves. They happen when peristalsis – waves of muscular contraction and relaxation that pass along the wall of the intestines – push liquid or air along the intestines.

Rumbling sounds

After eating a meal, hold the microphone steadily against your abdomen, record for two or three minutes, then play back the sounds.

Food provides the fuel for
all body activities

Food provides the body with the energy that cells need to work and stay alive. Carbohydrates, such as glucose, and fats are especially rich in energy. The liver helps to process food and to balance the level of nutrients in the blood.

Releasing energy

Inside all body cells there are tiny sausage-shaped structures called mitochondria. They take the glucose from food and release the energy stored in it. That energy is then used to power the processes that run, repair and maintain cells.

Energy
keeps the
cell alive

Glucose
from the
food we eat

Oxygen
from the air
we breathe

**Carbon
dioxide**
carried to the
lungs and
breathed out

Using energy

Our energy needs depend on how old we are and our sex. Growing children and teenagers, for example, use up much more energy daily than older people.

Power plants

We can be active because of what is happening inside the mitochondria in our cells.

Energy from food

Energy is measured in kilojoules (kJ) or in kilocalories (kcal) – 1 kcal = 4.2 kJ. Cheese, for example, contains more kilojoules or kilocalories (providing more energy) per gram than lettuce because it is high in fat – an energy-rich food. However, for a balanced diet we need to eat a range of foods that give us energy, but also the right balance of nutrients. How much energy we need each day depends on a number of things – including how active we are. A footballer, for example, uses more energy during a match than someone does playing football on a games console.

Busy liver

The liver performs over 500 jobs. Its millions of cells – called hepatocytes – process newly-digested food just after it has been absorbed. This makes sure that levels of energy-rich glucose, and other nutrients in the blood, stay balanced. They also remove poisons from the blood, store vitamins and minerals and release heat (see panel below).

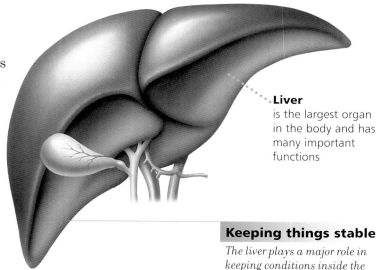

Liver
is the largest organ in the body and has many important functions

Keeping things stable
The liver plays a major role in keeping conditions inside the body the same at all times.

Out of balance

The body has a natural, long-term energy store. It is the fat found under the skin and in other places. But if we take in more energy in food than we use, the extra energy is stored as fat. If we stay out of balance – too much energy eaten, too little used – the fat stores increase and we put on weight. In the long term this can affect our health. The answer is to eat less fatty food and exercise often.

Overweight
Eating too much junk food and not exercising properly can lead to weight gain, and eventually obesity.

KEEPING WARM

The energy-releasing processes provide an important by-product: heat. Heat keeps the inside of your body at a temperature of 37°C (98.6°F), perfect for your cells to work at their best. You also have other ways of keeping to 37°C. If your surroundings are too hot, you take off some clothes and start sweating to cool down. If it is very cold, you wear more clothes and shiver to generate extra heat.

Too cold
Extra clothes, such as a jacket, hat and gloves, help to keep this snowboarder warm.

We can reduce the chances of food
making us ill

Without food and drink we cannot survive, but sometimes they give us something that is both extra and unwanted. Food and drink can carry bacteria and other germs that could make us very ill. However, there are various ways of reducing the chances of this happening.

Causing diseases
Food poisoning occurs when we eat food infected by bacteria or other germs, including viruses and protists. Symptoms include vomiting and diarrhoea, and generally feeling unwell. Buying good food from clean sources and keeping it properly, for example in the fridge, reduces the chances of infection.

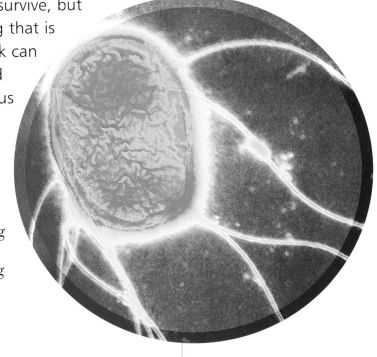

Salt preserving
Treating foods, such as meat, with salt stops them from 'going bad'. Bacteria and other germs cannot survive.

Unwanted germs
Bacteria, like this one, and other germs including viruses and protists, can quickly infect food that is not kept properly.

Raw or cooked?
Some foods, such as certain fruits and vegetables, are best eaten raw because they taste better and cooking may cause them to lose important vitamins. But other foods, such as potatoes and meat, should be properly cooked. Cooking food correctly makes it easier to digest and also kills bacteria and other germs on or in it.

Preserving food
To remain fit to eat over a period of time food is preserved. This makes sure it does not rot or become contaminated by harmful germs. Freezing kills some bacteria and stops others from reproducing. Chilling does the same, but for a shorter time. Salting, drying and pickling foods makes conditions too harsh for germs to survive.

CHOLERA EPIDEMICS

Cholera is a disease caused by drinking, or eating food washed in, water infected by bacteria. It results in severe vomiting and diarrhoea and can kill its victims. In the early 19th century there were several major cholera outbreaks in Europe and North America. Then people knew little about how diseases spread. But, in time it was realised that water polluted by sewage was causing the problem. With better drains and sewers, the disease disappeared – although outbreaks can still occur, mainly in developing countries, where open sewers are still common.

Open sewer

In parts of some developing countries, sewage is still carried by open ditches like this one. Open sewers increase the risk of disease, such as cholera.

Personal hygiene

The bacteria that live in our large intestine are helpful to us (see page 19). But these bacteria pass out of the body in faeces when we go to the toilet. Once outside the body, these once-friendly bacteria may become harmful and capable of causing disease if they get transferred to the mouth. That is why it is important to wash our hands after going to the toilet and before eating.

Washing hands

Using warm water and soap reduces the number of bacteria carried on the hands.

The kidneys remove waste and excess
water from the body

Body cells produce waste, like any busy factory, that must be removed from the body before they poison it. Removing waste is the job of the kidneys and the rest of the urinary system. They also get rid of any water and salt that entered the body in food or drink, but that is not needed.

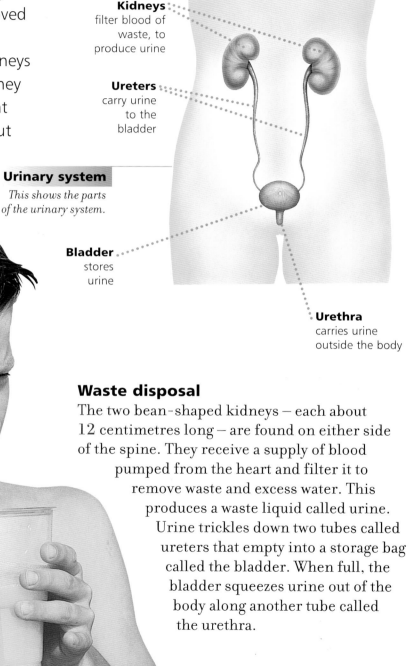

Kidneys
filter blood of waste, to produce urine

Ureters
carry urine to the bladder

Urinary system
This shows the parts of the urinary system.

Bladder
stores urine

Urethra
carries urine outside the body

Waste disposal

The two bean-shaped kidneys – each about 12 centimetres long – are found on either side of the spine. They receive a supply of blood pumped from the heart and filter it to remove waste and excess water. This produces a waste liquid called urine. Urine trickles down two tubes called ureters that empty into a storage bag called the bladder. When full, the bladder squeezes urine out of the body along another tube called the urethra.

Continuous cycle

Water is a major part of the liquids we drink and without it we would not survive for long. Water makes up most of the liquid in cells, blood and other body fluids. This water is being lost constantly.

Kidneys at work

Each kidney contains about one million microscopic tubes called nephrons, which act as filters. Liquid containing water, waste and simple nutrients is filtered out of the blood by the nephrons. As this fluid flows along the nephron tube the 'good' things, such as glucose and other simple nutrients, that the body needs are taken back into the blood. The 'bad' things, such as excess water and salts, flow in urine into the centre of the kidney and then into the ureter.

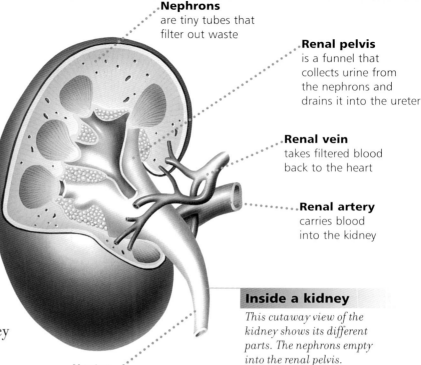

Nephrons
are tiny tubes that filter out waste

Renal pelvis
is a funnel that collects urine from the nephrons and drains it into the ureter

Renal vein
takes filtered blood back to the heart

Renal artery
carries blood into the kidney

Ureter
carries urine to the bladder

Inside a kidney

This cutaway view of the kidney shows its different parts. The nephrons empty into the renal pelvis.

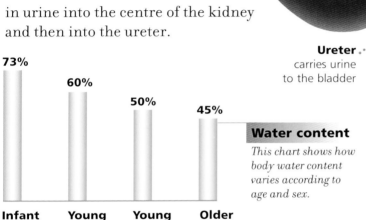

73% Infant
60% Young man
50% Young woman
45% Older person

Water content

This chart shows how body water content varies according to age and sex.

Water levels

To make the body work at its best, the kidneys balance its water content automatically, but we must keep drinking to replace fluid. The amount of water the body contains depends on age, sex and levels of body fat.

KIDNEY DIALYSIS

Sometimes a person's kidneys are so damaged by disease or injury that they stop filtering the blood and making urine. Today, these people can be treated by a process called kidney dialysis. The person's blood is pumped through a machine that contains membranes. These act like a real kidney and clean the blood. People with kidney problems need to have dialysis regularly, often several times a week.

Saving lives

Without a kidney dialysis machine to 'clean' her blood, this person would not survive.

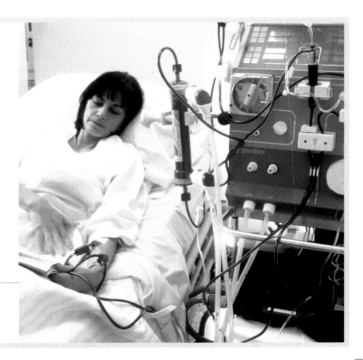

The bladder stores urine until it is ready
to be released

Going to the toilet to urinate – release urine – is a normal part of everyday life. As the kidneys make urine, the bladder stores it until we decide to urinate. Water lost in urine must be replaced by water from food and drink to make sure the body always has enough water inside it.

Ureters
connect the kidneys to the bladder

Expanding bag
This cutaway view of the bladder shows its very muscular, elastic wall.

Bladder

The bladder is an elastic storage bag with muscular walls that can expand from the size of a plum to a grapefruit as it fills with urine, and back again as it empties. Without a bladder we would release a constant dribble of urine to the outside of the body, making normal life impossible. The muscular ureters squeeze urine into the bladder. The exit from the bladder into the urethra – the tube that carries urine outside the body – is normally closed off by a ring of muscle called a sphincter.

Wall of muscle
expands and contracts as it fills and empties

Sphincter
controls the release of urine from the bladder

Filling and emptying

As urine flows down the two ureters from the kidneys, the bladder gradually fills and expands. Sensors in the bladder wall send nerve impulses to the brain and we feel the need to urinate. When convenient, we relax the sphincter muscle at the base of the bladder and the urine flows out, pushed by contraction of the bladder's muscular wall.

Releasing urine
These coloured x-rays show the difference in size between a full bladder (top) and an empty bladder (right).

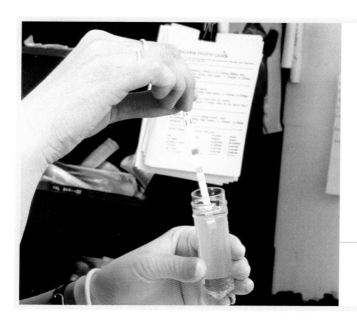

COLOUR, TASTE AND SMELL

In medieval times, doctors examined a patient's urine to find out what was wrong. They took a sample of urine in a glass flask and then checked up to 30 different features including its colour, taste and smell. Today, nurses take urine samples, but do not taste or smell them any more! Instead they rely on special chemical tests to find out if anything is wrong.

Urine test
A nurse examines urine using an indicator stick that will show her if anything is wrong.

Learning control

Until babies are about two years old they cannot control the sphincter muscles at the bottom of the bladder and rectum. Until they learn how to do this, they wear nappies to soak up the urine and faeces that are released every so often. Some elderly people can lose control of the bladder sphincter as they get older. This is called incontinence.

Essential nappies
Nappies are essential until a child learns to control its sphincters.

In and out
These charts show how 1200 millilitres of water lost each day is balanced by water gained.

Water Gained
Water in drinks	750 ml
Water in food	450 ml

Water Lost
Water in urine	600 ml
Water from lungs	200 ml
Water from skin	200 ml
Water in faeces	100 ml
Water in sweat	100 ml

Water balance

How much water the body contains (see pages 24–25) is controlled automatically. In this way, water gained by the body in food and drink is precisely balanced by water 'lost' by the body. Urination is not the only way water is lost. Water is also lost in sweat, faeces and in breathed-out air. If too much water is lost we feel thirsty, but can quickly make up the loss by drinking water.

Eating a balanced diet can
make us healthier

Imagine living on just baked beans, or surviving every day by only eating carrots. Not only would it make life very boring, but we would also be very ill. Fortunately, we are able to eat an enormous variety of food. The important thing is to make sure that what we eat gives us the right balance of nutrients (see pages 6–7).

(see pages 6–7)

Round the world

These meals from around the world include pizza from Italy, risotto from the Mediterranean, roast chicken and potato from North America and tofu and noodles from East Asia (right). They all contain a balance of nutrients.

Balanced diet

Although the word 'diet' is used to refer to losing weight, it simply means 'the food we eat daily'. A balanced diet is one that gives us the right mix of nutrients to keep us healthy. These can be obtained from a range of different foods that also provide us with vitamins, minerals and fibre.

Balancing act

A food pyramid organizes foods according to the nutrients they contain and how much we need to eat. The largest section shows foods that we need most of, such as carbohydrates. Foods that we need less of, such as those rich in fats and sugar, are shown in the smaller segments.

Diet guides

This pyramid gives a guide to how much of each food we should eat. The pie chart below shows the types of nutrient in a balanced diet.

30 per cent (maximum) fats

15 per cent proteins

55 per cent carbohydrates

Junk food

Junk food, or fast food, such as burgers, french fries and deep-fried chicken, are convenient because they avoid the need to prepare and cook food, such as the noodles and vegetables on the left. Eaten occasionally, junk food presents no problem. But eaten daily these foods do not give us a healthy balanced diet. They often contain high levels of fat, sugar and salt that we do not need, and low levels of vitamins and minerals which we do need.

Fast food

Eaten every day, fast food like this burger and fries gives us much more fat and salt than we need.

FOOD FOR HEALTH

Your daily diet should contain at least five portions of fruit and vegetables. Chilled, canned, frozen, fresh, dried fruit and vegetables, and 100 per cent juice all count. A balanced diet, combined with plenty of regular exercise, helps to make you fitter and healthier.

Good eating habits

School dinners give pupils, like these, a choice of food from a young age. But are the choices they are making giving them a balanced diet?

Glossary

Bacteria Group of living things, some of which cause diseases, that each consists of one simple cell.

Balanced diet A diet that contains a wide range of foods, in the right amounts, that allows the body to work properly and stay healthy.

Carbohydrates Group of substances, which include sugars and starches, that are the body's main energy source.

Cell One of trillions of tiny living units that make up the human body.

Chyme Soup-like liquid containing part-digested food, released from the stomach into the small intestine during digestion.

Dehydrated Describes a person whose water content is less than it should be.

Diet The type and amount of food a person eats each day.

Enamel Very hard material that covers the top of a tooth.

Endoscope Instrument used by doctors to look inside the body.

Enzyme Substance that greatly speeds up the breakdown of food during digestion.

Fats Group of substances found in foods that supply the body with energy and help to insulate it.

Fibre Material found in plant foods that cannot be digested but makes the intestine's muscles work more efficiently.

Gastric Describes things that are part of, or are made by, the stomach.

Germs General term for microscopic living things (micro-organisms), such as viruses and some bacteria, that cause diseases.

Gland Group of cells that release substances into, or onto, the body.

Gums Soft tissues that cover the jawbones and surround the teeth.

Minerals Group of 20 substances, including iron and calcium, that must be present in a person's diet to maintain good health.

Mitochondria (singular: mitochondrion) Sausage-shaped components of cells that carry out cell respiration to release energy from food.

Molecule A simple chemical structure.

Mucus Thick, slippery liquid produced by the lining of the digestive system.

Nutrients Substances in food – such as carbohydrates, proteins, fats, minerals, or vitamins – needed by the body to work properly.

Obesity Condition in which the body's weight is greater than normal because of excess fat stores.

Organ Body part, such as the stomach, that is made up of two or more types of tissues and which has a specific job to do.

Peristalsis Wave of muscle contraction that pushes food along the oesophagus and intestines.

Plaque Deposit of food and bacteria that builds up on teeth if they are not brushed properly.

Proteins Group of substances used by the body for growth and repair, and to make enzymes.

Protists Group of single-celled organisms, a few of which cause diseases in humans.

Pulp Soft tissue inside teeth, containing blood vessels and nerves.

Saliva Digestive liquid released into the mouth that helps food slip down the throat.

Sewage Water that contains human faeces and other waste.

Sphincter Ring of muscle around an opening that opens and closes to control the flow of, for example, urine.

Tissues Collection of the same, or similar, cells that work together to perform a specific task.

Urea Waste substance produced in the liver and removed from the blood by the kidneys.

Urinate To release urine from the body.

Urine Liquid made by the kidneys that contains wastes, such as urea, and excess water.

Villi (singular villus) Tiny, finger-like projections from the wall of the small intestine that absorb nutrients.

Virus One of a group of living particles that cause diseases in humans and other living things.

Vitamins A group of over 13 substances, including vitamins C and D, needed in small amounts in a person's diet to make the body work normally.

Find out more

These are just some of the websites where you can find out more information about how we digest food. Many of the websites also provide information and illustrations about other systems and processes of the human body.

Note to parents and teachers
Every effort has been made by the Publishers to ensure that these websites are suitable for children; that they are of the highest educational value, and that they contain no inappropriate or offensive material. However, because of the nature of the Internet, it is impossible to guarantee that the contents of these sites will not be altered. We strongly advise that Internet access is supervised by a responsible adult.

www.kidshealth.org/kid/body/mybody_SW.html
Tells you lots more about your teeth, tongue, kidneys and digestive system.

http://yucky.kids.discovery.com/flash/body/pg000029.html
This website provides gross information about the digestive and urinary systems.

www.exhibits.pacsci.org/nutrition/
Join in activities to do with food and eating, such as 'Have-a-Bite' and 'Nutrition Café'.

www.hyperstaffs.info/science/work/dargavel/index.htm
Follow the adventures of Yasmin and Jack at the dentist to learn more about looking after your teeth.

www.galaxy-h.gov.uk
This website lets you choose your school meals and find out information about what you have selected.

http://vilenski.org/science/humanbody
Join in the 'Human Body Adventure' to find out more about the digestive and urinary systems.

www.brainpop.com/health/digestive/
This website features movies and quizzes about food, digestion, teeth, body weight and lots more.

www.james.com/beaumont/dr_life.htm
Find out about the American surgeon William Beaumont and his digestive experiments on Alexis St Martin (see page 15).

http://web.ukonline.co.uk/webwise/spinneret/other/anenz.htm
This webpage has an animation that shows how enzymes work.

www.amnh.org/national-center/infection/
Click on 'Bacteria in the Cafeteria' to discover more about food and germs.

www.medtropolis.com/VBody.asp
Provides an animated guided tour of the digestive system.

www.nutritionaustralia.org
A website featuring information about nutritional values and food labels and facts.

www.kellogg.com.au/nutritioninfo/listnutritioninfo.asp
Helps to explain a variety of cereal food nutrition panels.

Index